HARRIS COUNTY PUBLIC LIBRARY

W9-BJK-720

At Issue

| Are Women Paid Fairly?

Other Books in the At Issue Series:

At Issue

I Are Women Paid Fairly?

Jennifer Dorman

GREENHAVEN PRESS

A part of Gale, Cengage Learning

GALE
CENGAGE Learning·

Detroit • New York • San Francisco • New Haven, Conn • Waterville, Maine • London

GALE
CENGAGE Learning·

Elizabeth Des Chenes, *Director, Publishing Solutions*

© 2013 Greenhaven Press, a part of Gale, Cengage Learning

Gale and Greenhaven Press are registered trademarks used herein under license.

For more information, contact:
Greenhaven Press
27500 Drake Rd.
Farmington Hills, MI 48331-3535
Or you can visit our Internet site at gale.cengage.com

For product information and technology assistance, contact us at

Gale Customer Support, 1-800-877-4253
For permission to use material from this text or product, submit all requests online at www.cengage.com/permissions

Further permissions questions can be emailed to permissionrequest@cengage.com

Articles in Greenhaven Press anthologies are often edited for length to meet page requirements. In addition, original titles of these works are changed to clearly present the main thesis and to explicitly indicate the author's opinion. Every effort is made to ensure that Greenhaven Press accurately reflects the original intent of the authors. Every effort has been made to trace the owners of copyrighted material.

Cover image copyright © Images.com/Corbis.

LIBRARY OF CONGRESS CATALOGING-IN-PUBLICATION DATA

Are women paid fairly? / Jennifer Dorman, book editor.
    p. cm. -- (At issue)
Includes bibliographical references and index.
   ISBN 978-0-7377-6153-5 (hbk.) -- ISBN 978-0-7377-6154-2 (pbk.)
   1. Equal pay for equal work. 2. Wages--Women. 3. Pay equity. 4. Discrimination in employment. 5. Women--Employment. I. Dorman, Jennifer.
   HD6061.A74 2013
   331.4'2153--dc23

                          2012030794

Printed in the United States of America
1 2 3 4 5   16 15 14 13 12

Contents

Introduction

Lilly Ledbetter worked at Goodyear Tire and Rubber Co. nearly 20 years before discovering that she had been a victim of gender-based wage discrimination. Armed with two important pieces of legislation protecting women from such discrimination, The Equal Pay Act of 1963 and the Equal Rights Act of 1964 (Title VII), Ledbetter took Goodyear to court after her early retirement in 1998. A grandmother from Alabama and an unlikely activist, Ledbetter's story captured the public's imagination and made waves throughout the political and business world.

Ledbetter had served as an area manager in a position predominately held by men. She had previously signed a document saying that she would not discuss salaries with other workers at the plant, but before her early retirement in 1998, Ledbetter discovered that a pay disparity had developed between her and her male colleagues. This disparity affected her weekly salary, overtime pay, and 401K contributions. Says Ledbetter, "Going back in my career, in the early 1990s I was selected to be one of the four managers to start up the light-truck radial division and then in '96 I was given a top-performance award. It was just very humiliating to realize that I had been so undercut in my wages."[1]

Ledbetter decided to sue Goodyear for discriminatory practices. "I didn't want anybody to give me anything," says Ledbetter, "I didn't want any special treatment. I just wanted the opportunity to have the job, to do the job and to get compensated. And really, had it been close, had it just been close, I would have probably not pursued it because when you get into a charge of this nature it's not a quick fix."[2] It did indeed turn into a long journey. Though Ledbetter won her initial case, Goodyear appealed, ultimately to the Supreme Court. In 2007 Ledbetter's case was overturned in a 5-4 decision because she did not file her suit in a timely matter. The court admitted that she was a victim of discrimination but ruled her claim exceeded the 180-day statute of limitations.

In her dissent, Judge Ruth Ginsberg made it clear why she disagreed with the ruling:

> The problem of concealed pay discrimination is particularly acute where the disparity arises not because the female employee is flatly denied a raise but because male counterparts are given larger raises. Having received a pay increase, the female employee is unlikely to discern at once that she has experienced an adverse employment decision. She may have little reason even to suspect discrimination until a pattern develops incrementally and she ultimately becomes aware of the disparity. Even if an employee suspects that the reason for a comparatively low raise is not performance but sex (or another protected ground), the amount involved may seem too small, or the employer's intent too ambiguous, to make the issue immediately actionable—or winnable."[3]

With this ammunition, congressional democrats—including then presidential hopeful Barack Obama—took up her cause in 2008, and on January 29, 2009, President Obama signed the Lilly Ledbetter Fair Pay Act into law, his first piece of legislation. The Act states that the 180-day clock for filing a wage disparity claim resets with each discriminatory pay check.

While many celebrated this event, others saw it as a blow to businesses. One vocal opponent of the legislation was the American Hotel and Lodging Association (AH&LA):

> Because the bill virtually eliminates any time limitations for claims of employment discrimination, expands the pool of potential claimants and is vaguely written which would encourage predatory legal claims to exploit its vague language, AH&LA strongly opposes this bill.[4]

Congressman Tom McClintock was also outspoken in his opposition, focusing on the highly variable nature of employer/employee negotiations:

Imposing rigid one-size-fits-all requirements into the relationship between an employee and an employer reduces the employee's freedom to negotiate for the best set of conditions for his or her own unique circumstances.

And lest we forget, when all else fails there is a fail-safe and absolute protection the market provides to all: it is the word, "no." "No, the pay isn't acceptable;" "No, the conditions aren't satisfactory;" "No, I can get a better offer elsewhere."[5]

The question of a male-female wage gap is a volatile subject and people have vastly differing opinions about the issue. Many find the gender wage gap an anachronistic reality that must be eradicated, while others find that there are good, solid reasons for the disparity. The discussion about the wage gap between men and women is particularly topical due to the passage of the Lilly Ledbetter Fair Pay Act and the rejection by congress of the Paycheck Fairness Act. *At Issue: Are Women Paid Fairly?* examines various viewpoints as to whether the wage disparity is based on sexual discrimination, women's choices, or a variety of other factors.

Notes

1. Kate Connelly, "An Ordinary Human Being Can Make a Difference," www.thedailybeast.com, January 29, 2009.
2. Kate Connelly, "An Ordinary Human Being Can Make a Difference," www.thedailybeast.com, January 29, 2009.
3. Ginsburg, J., dissenting, Supreme Court of the United States, *Lilly M. Ledbetter, Petitioner v. The Goodyear Tire & Rubber Company, Inc.*, on writ of certiorari to the united states court of appeals for the eleventh circuit [May 29, 2007].
4. American Hotel & Lodging Association, Government Advisory: Congress Is Back, and They Need to Hear from You: Oppose the "Paycheck Fairness Act" and "Lilly Ledbetter Fair Pay Act," August 1, 2009.
5. Tom McClintock, "Speech in Opposition to S181—Lilly Ledbetter Salary Act," January 27, 2009.

1

Don't Get Mad, Get Even

Ann Crittenden

Ann Crittenden is the author of The Price of Motherhood and
If You've Raised Kids, You Can Manage Anything.

*The gender wage gap exists because women are not paid fairly.
The following viewpoint argues that fair wages are still an elusive dream for working women. Women are now essentially even
with men in terms of education and experience, yet men are still
paid more and tend to do better in the workplace than women.
The book* Getting Even *is a constant reminder that the battle for
fair wages still has not been won for women.*

*Getting Even: Why Women Don't Get Paid Like Men—And
What To Do About It* by Evelyn Murphy with E.J. Graff
(Touchstone, 352 pages, $24.95)

Just when you thought the news couldn't get any worse, here
comes a report from the trenches of the American workplace, where apparently women are still being short-changed
in the same old egregious ways. I must admit that I had
thought that blatant, in-your-face sex discrimination was by
and large a thing of the past, except in a few dark corners of
male chauvinism like Wall Street, the extractive industries, the
skilled trades, Hooters, and your neighborhood garage. You
know, where things are filthy with lucre or grease or grime.

But no, no such luck. A new and damning report by Evelyn Murphy, former lieutenant governor of Massachusetts, makes it clear that fair wages are still an elusive dream, even for women working full time, shoulder to shoulder with the boys. As Murphy documents, the reality in every imaginable occupation can be a nightmare.

Getting Even, co-authored by E.J. Graff, is a litany of abuses, many culled from the records of discrimination lawsuits that were settled in favor of the plaintiffs. We meet the ambitious young police officer who was completely sidelined after her second pregnancy. The woman whose investment banker boss stuffed money in her bra and asked for oral sex. The endocrinologist who found she was earning 24 percent less than her male colleague with less seniority. The chemical worker who was severely harassed by co-workers led by a ringleader who believed the Bible intended women to be subject to male authority. He was promoted and she had to quit. And on and on, in numbing, depressing, convincing detail.

One could be skeptical about the significance of this kind of anecdotal data, but no one can deny the arresting fact that for several years in the 1990s, the gender wage gap between full-time working men and women stopped its slow process of narrowing and actually widened. By 2003, women were still earning only 77 cents to the men's dollar. Even among young male and female college graduates, starting salaries were further apart in 2003 than they had been in 1991. (The women earned 16 percent less in their first job than the men, versus 9 percent less in 1991.) Young women with only a high school degree slipped even further behind. By 2003, those working full-time in the "pink-collar ghetto" earned 22 percent less than blue-collar young men, compared with 18 percent less in 1991.

The only group of women who narrowed the gender wage gap during the 1990s was those with graduate degrees. Women between the ages of 35 and 44 with degrees in law, business, and medicine who were working full time narrowed the gap with comparable men from 29 percent to 14 percent between 1991 and 2003. Since these are the women who tend to attract the most media attention, their relative success may have obscured the fact that many more millions of women are dropping further behind.

What on earth is going on? Women have now essentially drawn even with men in education and experience. Murphy cites economist Heidi Hartmann's observation that when times are good, men tend to do better than women. And indeed, men's wages in the booming '90s did rise faster than those of comparable women. By any definition, that ain't fair. Worse, the country accepts this systematic unfairness as a given. Murphy reports that when she asked people what women ought to be earning compared with men, most said they had no idea, or guessed that women should earn about 80 cents to a man's $1. No one thought the answer should be equal pay for equal work.

Women have now essentially drawn even with men in education and experience.

This passivity may help explain why women continue to lag: They are not demanding their fair share. And that is incredibly costly both to them and to those who share their lives, including most men and almost all children. Lifetime earnings losses due to the gender wage gap alone can amount to more than $1 million for a college graduate and $700,000 for a high school graduate. That translates into a more impoverished or insecure old age and more bankruptcies among women. It means more modest housing, fewer vacations, and above all, greater anxiety about paying the bills, including those for children's higher education. Murphy is eager to convey these personal costs in this book. She constantly reminds readers what they could buy with that money they never earn, asking at one point, "Why would any hard-working, able woman willingly forego making as much money as she possibly could?"

Well, actually, there's a reason. Millions of able hard-working women do forego making as much money as they possibly can in order to have more time for life. Murphy doesn't mention that full-time working women don't work as many hours as full-time working men, which surely explains some of the gender wage gap. And her analysis leaves out fully half of all working age women with children, because they don't work full time; they work part time or not at all for money. They pay an even heavier economic price, but do so because they are more concerned about time poverty than relative wage poverty.

This does not mean that they willingly choose to be economically marginalized. Many if not most did not really "opt out" as often described; they were pushed out, edged out, sidelined, or derailed. Indeed, if the myriad forms of discrimination and harassment Murphy documents were reduced or eliminated, I have no doubt that countless women who are currently out of the labor force or working part time would return, to the enormous benefit of their pocketbooks.

After decades of denial that feminism has any relevance today, women have to face the fact that unless they stand up, speak out, and maybe even pick a fight, things are not going to get better and could easily get worse.

But by essentially ignoring the other great problem women face in the workplace—time pressure—Murphy limits the appeal of her message. She says nothing of the need for more humane working hours, for paid sick days and parental leaves. Unmentioned is the need to eliminate mandatory overtime and to establish parity of pay and benefits for part-time workers, most of whom are women. She is dead right in insisting that nothing is going to change until women themselves demand it, but I suspect that as a childless woman who has always been a flat-out professional, she misjudges the preference that many women have for a less work-centered existence. John de Graaf, the founder of the Take Back Your Time movement, likes to remind people that when thousands of women walked off their jobs in the textile mills of Lawrence, Massachusetts, during the massive strike of 1912, they carried signs demanding "bread and roses"—higher wages and shorter hours. These were the two great goals of the original labor movement: money and time to smell the roses.

Still, *Getting Even* is an extremely useful reminder that fair wages for women is a battle that is still not won. After decades of denial that feminism has any relevance today, women have to face the fact that unless they stand up, speak out, and maybe even pick a fight, things are not going to get better and could easily get worse. Not content with just writing a book, Murphy has also launched The WAGE (Women Are Getting Even) Project Inc., dedicated to closing the gender wage gap in 10 years. I clicked on the Web site (www.wageproject.org) and found a place where you can type in your salary and then discover what the average male in the same position, same industry, and same region was earning, based on year 2000 data. I put in a $25,000 income for a hypothetical secretary in financial services in Montgomery County, Maryland. (I didn't dare to put in freelance writer). Back came the information that 95 percent of the people in that job were female, and that this hypothetical woman's salary was 56 percent of that of a male in the same job.

2

There Is No Male-Female Wage Gap

Carrie Lukas

Carrie Lukas is the Executive Director of the Independent Women's Forum.

Wages are not the only factor in job choice. Discussion of a male/female wage gap does not take into account the myriad factors involved in job choice and compensation. The recent economic downturn has shed light on a number of factors that variously affect both men and women. Women experienced fewer job losses during the recession because they tend to choose jobs in more stable industries. In general, women trade higher pay for job security and a safer work environment. Women also earn less than men because they work fewer hours.

Tuesday is Equal Pay Day—so dubbed by the National Committee for Pay Equity, which represents feminist groups including the National Organization for Women, Feminist Majority, the National Council of Women's Organizations and others. The day falls on April 12 because, according to feminist logic, women have to work that far into a calendar year before they earn what men already earned the year before.

In years past, feminist leaders marked the occasion by rallying outside the U.S. Capitol to decry the pernicious wage gap and call for government action to address systematic discrimination against women. This year will be relatively quiet. Perhaps feminists feel awkward protesting a liberal-dominated government—or perhaps they know that the recent economic downturn has exposed as ridiculous their claims that our economy is ruled by a sexist patriarchy.

The unemployment rate is consistently higher among men than among women. The Bureau of Labor Statistics reports that 9.3% of men over the age of 16 are currently out of work. The figure for women is 8.3%. Unemployment fell for both sexes over the past year, but labor force participation (the percentage of working age people employed) also dropped. The participation rate fell more among men (to 70.4% today from 71.4% in March 2010) than women (to 58.3% from 58.8%). That means much of the improvement in unemployment numbers comes from discouraged workers— particularly male ones—giving up their job searches entirely.

Men have been hit harder by this recession because they tend to work in fields like construction, manufacturing and trucking, which are disproportionately affected by bad economic conditions. Women cluster in more insulated occupations, such as teaching, health care and service industries.

Yet if you can accept that the job choices of men and women lead to different unemployment rates, then you shouldn't be surprised by other differences—like differences in average pay.

Feminist hand-wringing about the wage gap relies on the assumption that the differences in average earnings stem from discrimination. Thus the mantra that women make only 77% of what men earn for equal work. But even a cursory review of the data proves this assumption false.

The Department of Labor's Time Use survey shows that full-time working women spend an average of 8.01 hours per day on the job, compared to 8.75 hours for full-time working men. One would expect that someone who works 9%

more would also earn more. This one fact alone accounts for more than a third of the wage gap.

Choice of occupation also plays an important role in earnings. While feminists suggest that women are coerced into lower-paying job sectors, most women know that something else is often at work. Women gravitate toward jobs with fewer risks, more comfortable conditions, regular hours, more personal fulfillment and greater flexibility. Simply put, many women—not all, but enough to have a big impact on the statistics—are willing to trade higher pay for other desirable job characteristics.

Men, by contrast, often take on jobs that involve physical labor, outdoor work, overnight shifts and dangerous conditions (which is also why men suffer the overwhelming majority of injuries and deaths at the workplace). They put up with these unpleasant factors so that they can earn more.

[M]any women ... are willing to trade higher pay for other desirable job characteristics.

Recent studies have shown that the wage gap shrinks—or even reverses—when relevant factors are taken into account and comparisons are made between men and women in similar circumstances. In a 2010 study of single, childless urban workers between the ages of 22 and 30, the research firm Reach Advisors found that women earned an average of 8% more than their male counterparts. Given that women are outpacing men in educational attainment, and that our economy is increasingly geared toward knowledge-based jobs, it makes sense that women's earnings are going up compared to men's.

Should we celebrate the closing of the wage gap? Certainly it's good news that women are increasingly productive workers, but women whose husbands and sons are out of work or under-employed are likely to have a different perspective. After all, many American women wish they could work less, and that they weren't the primary earners for their families.

Few Americans see the economy as a battle between the sexes. They want opportunity to abound so that men and women can find satisfying work situations that meet their unique needs. That—not a day dedicated to manufactured feminist grievances—would be something to celebrate.

3

Young Women Are Increasingly Paid More than Young Men

Gaby Hinsliff

The former political editor of the Observer, *Gaby Hinsliff is a writer, blogger, and broadcaster on public policy and private lives.*

Due to increased education, inherent skills, and a basic increase in the value of women in the workplace, young women are beginning to out-earn their male counterparts. While this development threatens the traditional gender model, wage fairness benefits society as a whole and should be celebrated. It is unclear whether this trend can continue for women through their childbearing years.

It is not often, in these dark times, that one stumbles across a snippet of good economic news. So it's strange that one such shaft of sunlight in the gloom has gone mostly unsung. According to official statistics released last week [November, 2011], *the pay gap between men and women*—that barometer of shifting power between the sexes—has quietly shrunk to a record low and among younger women has shot clearly into reverse. Women in their 20s now earn a solid 3.6% more on average than men their age, after narrowly overtaking them for the first time last year [2010]. The rise of the female bread-winner, it seems, was no blip, but the beginning perhaps of a social and sexual sea change.

Some Are Threatened by Women's Rising Wages

For an angry but vocal minority, that is a change too far, yet more proof that they are the underdogs now, trampled beneath the stilettoes of supposedly over-mighty women. The conservative family policy expert Jill Kirby even suggested that "the *pay* gap we should be worrying about is the one that shows young men falling behind", not the one that still sees men earning more than women for every other decade of their working life.

Losing ground is admittedly never easy, even if that ground wasn't always earned, as one glance at the Tory [UK political party] backbenches, boiling with resentment at young women being promoted over older male heads, confirms. The trouble with shattering the glass ceiling is that someone inevitably ends up ducking the flying fragments.

Once They Were Threatened by Women's Lower Wages

But it's worth remembering that, barely a century ago, the great male fear was not of alpha females with intimidatingly large salaries but their polar opposite: women were seen, rather like immigrant labour now, as dangerously liable to undercut men's wages by doing the same work for less. Equal pay was sold not as a threat but, rather intriguingly, as a promise.

As the then mayor of New York put it in 1911, explaining his decision to grant 14,000 female teachers the same salaries as men: "Instead of lessening the number of male teachers this will increase it" by removing the financial incentive to hire women. Even in 1946, the Royal Commission on Equal Pay set up in Britain argued that *equality* would mean women losing their jobs, since "at equal pay for men and women, a man will always be preferred". Why on earth would you hire a woman, unless she was going cheap?

Can Women Celebrate Their Achievement?

Half a century on, it seems incredibly mean-spirited not to allow young women at least a moment's triumph over proving such arguments wrong, before making them hang their heads in shame for the men they have left behind. But instead, the same reproachful message has been drummed into them since their teens, when they outstripped boys at GCSE [General Certificate of Secondary Education—offered in a variety of subjects, GCSEs are the main academic qualification taken by British Students, ages 14–16] and A-level [Advanced Level—A-levels are courses taken by British Students to qualify for university] only to face howls of protest about education being rigged in their favour.

It's not that this argument was without any merit. Where boys are failing, schools should question what's happening in the classroom. It's just depressing that the debate so often contrived to make young girls' strengths—greater social confidence and maturity or a conscientiousness that makes them better at coursework—sound strangely like cheating, since these skills have turned out to be undeniably handy.

After all, those same girls went on to beat boys at degree level, to form the majority of trainee barristers and solicitors and fast-track civil servants by the middle of the last decade. They're the same girls who, a graduate recruiter once told me, shone so much at interview that they left the boys standing.

And they grew up into the same junior managers who, according to a recent survey for the Chartered Management Institute [CMI], now out-earn their male counterparts for the first time since 1974. Even if the pay gap between senior executives still yawns so wide that the CMI estimates it will take a century to close, they must have been doing something right.

The Wage Gap Varies Directly with Women's Age

What is emerging now is a striking generational divide. The pay gap for full-time workers is biggest now for women in their 50s—those least likely to have been encouraged when young to pursue a career or hang on to one after children. But it narrows with every decade subtracted from a woman's age.

Roughly speaking, as girls' horizons have widened and their skill sets swelled (only a quarter of girls went to university in the 1960s, for example, whereas by 1996 they outnumbered boys), their earning power has risen in tandem. Legislation, industrial action, a greater emphasis on traditionally "female" skills, such as communication, and sheer bloody-mindedness all helped.

Legislation, industrial action, a greater emphasis on traditionally "female" skills, such as communication, and sheer bloody-mindedness all helped.

Fairness Matters

But one reason young women now get paid more than their mothers is simply that they're worth it, a basic fairness that matters more to a cohesive society than perhaps we used to think.

After all, what fuels the festering anger at rocketing boardroom pay isn't just naked envy of the 4,000% increase in some top bosses' salaries over the past three decades, as the High Pay Commission reported, but a feeling that there's no rhyme nor reason to it. It's not as if their companies are thousands of times more profitable. And this breaking of the link between effort and reward is a profoundly unsettling thing: why strive to do your best if you get nothing while the undeserving merrily trouser their bonuses? Which is precisely how too many women have long felt about their male colleagues.

It's easy to forget not just how stonkingly, grievously unfair things have been in the past, but also how tentative these female gains have been. Men who work full time still earn 9% more than women overall, hardly suggestive of being chucked on the scrapheap—any more than the existence of a measly five female cabinet ministers (outnumbered five to one by men) really spells matriarchy.

We don't even know yet whether this is merely a case of tortoise and hare, with young women shooting off to a confident start only to find themselves overtaken the minute they pause to have babies. After all, men's earnings start to outstrip women's from the age of 29—precisely when Mrs Average now has her first child.

It's far from clear that this generation of golden girls can beat the so-called "motherhood penalty", either by managing hitherto unsuspected feats of juggling or by persuading some of their lower-paid husbands to take on more at home. But at a time when hopes of future wage growth for anyone seem few and far between, perhaps we could at least stop hounding them for trying.

4

Men Reap the Benefits of Highly Paid Wives

Petula Dvorak

Petula Dvorak is a columnist for the Washington Post.

According to several surveys, men today are living well, partly thanks to their highly paid wives. Marriage used to provide financial safety for women, but it is now providing this function for many men as well. Women have made great strides in providing for their family financially, but men have not necessarily picked up the slack at home. Many women find themselves to be both the breadwinner and the primary domestic caretaker.

Things are sweeter than ever for the recliner kings of America's four-bedroom, two-and-a-half bath castles.

Contemporary American husbands are working less, going to school less, living longer and are reaping the benefits of wives who are bringing home the big bucks more than any of their dapper *Mad Men* counterparts of the 1960s.

It continues to be a man's world, only a little more comfy these days.

New Studies Point to Rise of Working Women

So say a barrage of new studies in the past few months that show women in America are just about to make up the *major-*

ity of the U.S. workforce, are dominating universities and now, in ever-increasing numbers, are the better-educated, more handsomely paid half of American marriages.

Okay, maybe I'm exaggerating a little, but all these recent studies are pointing to an interesting trend—marriage is increasingly becoming a better deal for the male of the species.

It continues to be a man's world, only a little more comfy these days.

The study released [on January 19, 2010] by the Pew Research Center shows that in one out of five married couples, the wife earns more than the husband. That's a huge shift in 40 years, when this was the case in just 4 percent of American marriages.

Men Are Reaping Financial Benefits of Marriage

It used to be that marriage was one of the big ways in which women got an economic boost, according to Pew researchers. Outside of fairytales where the scamp snags the baron's daughter, it was rarely the other way around.

But today, more men than ever better their lot by marrying a smart, career-driven woman.

This is a big change for a growing number of men whose dads were expected to support a cast of dependents after they walked down the aisle.

So on the whole, there's a little less pressure on men to financially carry the entire household today. That may not offer much solace to the men who have borne the brunt of the layoffs in this recession. In some marriages, those layoffs are the reason a woman is the principal breadwinner.

The Downside to Women's Workplace Success

But women have been making gains in the workplace for four decades—a shift that ought to be an indicator of fantastic social change. Only, in reality, women's increasing success is not so rosy up close.

The counterpoint to what Pew calls "the rise of wives" is another study entitled "The Paradox of Declining Female Happiness," which says that women, despite their huge social and economic leaps, aren't feeling all zippity-do-dah about life these days.

And that one should be pretty easy to figure out.

While earning more and working more, most women still have to do most of the stuff at home that they did before they got the corner office and the corporate bonus. Even those who can afford to hire help still work two or maybe two-and-a-half jobs.

Time-use surveys by the Bureau of Labor Statistics show that women still carry the bigger load of chores, household duties and child care and get less personal time than men.

And when a husband takes care of the kids, most folks (my husband included) call it "babysitting."

Women Still Do More Around the House

Husbands are picking up more of the household duties, as authors Betsey Stevenson and Justin Wolfers of the women-are-depressed study noted.

But they also pointed out that when men load the dishwasher, many people still say they are "helping out" at home (do you ever say a woman is "helping" when she does the laundry?). And when a husband takes care of the kids, most folks (my husband included) call it "babysitting."

We are a generation of working women trapped between two extremes.

There is the 1950s uber-mom, with the apron, the after-school cookies, the costumes sewn for the school play and the tucking in with a kiss every night. She couldn't be a career woman, that just wasn't done.

And then there's the 1980s power-mom, who was taught never to bring baked goods into the office, wore the woman-suit with the floppy bow tie, carried the briefcase and the tied the house key around the kid's neck with scratchy yarn. No need for a pot roast in the oven—they'd just invented the microwave!

So millennial mom is now expected to be both.

There is no excuse for her not to succeed at work, all those doors have been kicked open, right?

And millennial mom has to feed her kids all organic, homemade food. No more frozen chicken patties and Hamburger Helper late, late at night, right?

And the school keeps asking us to volunteer on the board, and we go on field trips while answering our BlackBerrys and sit at our desks while calling the preschool.

Whew.

Honey, can I get a turn on the recliner?

5

The Wage Gap Is the Result of Discrimination

Mashaun D. Simon

Mashaun D. Simon is a writer for Black Enterprise.

The following viewpoint discusses a bill to end gender pay discrimination that was still pending Senate approval in 2008. At the time of this article's publication, statistics claimed that on average, women earned only 77 percent of the amount men earned. The Payness Fairness Act would put gender-based wage discrimination on equal footing with other discriminations by allowing women to sue for punitive damages.

Women across America are claiming a small victory thanks to the passage of a bill designed to end gender-based pay discrimination. H.R. 1338, the Paycheck Fairness Act, still pending Senate approval, could make it easier for women to sue employers for wage bias.

The Paycheck Fairness Act takes immediate steps to close the wage gap for women by amending and strengthening the Equal Pay Act of 1963, according to Rep. Barbara Lee (D-Calif.), a cosponsor of the bill who spoke on the floor of the House of Representatives. "Although the wage gap between men and women has narrowed since the passage of the EPA, gender-based wage discrimination remains a problem for women in the U.S. workforce," Lee said in a statement.

According to the U.S. Bureau of Labor Statistics, women still earn on average only 77% of what men earn. The situation is far worse for women of color. For every dollar men earned in 2006, African American women were paid just 64 cents; Hispanic women earned 52 cents.

"The wage disparity between men and women costs women anywhere from $400,000 to $2 million over a lifetime—keenly impacting the economic security of single women who are heads of households and those women in retirement," adds Lee.

Based on AAUW research, just one year after college graduation, women earn only 80% of what their male counterparts earn.

Not even a college degree is much help, says Lisa M. Maatz, director of Public Policy and Government Relations at the American Association of University Women. Based on AAUW research, just one year after college graduation, women earn only 80% of what their male counterparts earn. As they move further up in their careers, women fall further behind, earning about 69% of what men earn 10 years after having graduated college.

Maatz says the Paycheck Fairness Act takes some basic yet meaningful steps. While it strengthens some of the loopholes of the EPA, it also puts some enforcement efforts into place. Most importantly, she says, it prohibits retaliation by employers against employees who speak out or even discuss their pay with colleagues. Moreover, it puts gender-based discrimination sanctions on equal footing with other forms of discrimination—such as discrimination based on race, disability, or age—by allowing women to sue for compensatory and punitive damages. The Paycheck Fairness Act would also increase the available penalties of companies found in violation of the law and provide additional training opportunities for Equal Employment Opportunity Commission staff to better identify and handle wage disputes.

It might have taken more than a decade, says Maatz, but a message has been sent by the House: "Gender-based pay discrimination will not be tolerated." Maatz hopes that, as law, the Paycheck Fairness Act will deter employers from unequal pay practices and encourage them to self-police.

But not all women see the necessity in H.R. 1338. "I am really scratching my head over why the Paycheck Fairness Act is a priority," says Deborah Stallings, president and CEO of HR ANEW, a minority- and woman-owned agency specializing in human resources management, compensation and benefits design and administration, employment law, management, recruitment, and hiring. "This problem [of gender-based pay discrimination] has improved greatly since the passage of the EPA."

As an HR consultant, Stallings says she's opposed to HR 1338 as it is currently written. However, "paying women and all people fairly is a marketplace issue, and I'm not opposed to an agenda that ensures that all people are paid fairly and equally based upon knowledge, skills, abilities, education, and other demographics such as geographical location, industry, etc."

Maatz says she urges the Senate to pass HR 1338. "Equal pay for equal work is a serious issue, and women are paying more attention in this election season."

6

The Wage Gap Is a Result of Women's Choices

Christina Hoff Sommers

Christina Hoff Sommers is a resident scholar at the American Enterprise Institute.

The latest proposal of a paycheck fairness bill is misguided, as it aligns with those who believe that a male-female wage gap exists as a result of discrimination against women. Any wage gap can be explained by many other factors, particularly individual choices. The bill would be unfair to employers and create an inaccurately bleak picture of women in the workplace.

Among the top items left on the Senate's to-do list before the November [2010] elections is a "paycheck fairness" bill [this bill, which would make it easier for women to file class-action, punitive-damages suits against employers they accuse of sex-based pay discrimination [The Paycheck Fairness Act did not pass].

The bill's passage is hardly certain, but it has received strong support from women's rights groups, professional organizations and even President Obama, who has called it "a common-sense bill."

But the bill isn't as commonsensical as it might seem. It overlooks mountains of research showing that discrimination plays little role in pay disparities between men and women, and it threatens to impose onerous requirements on employers to correct gaps over which they have little control.

The bill is based on the premise that the 1963 Equal Pay Act, which bans sex discrimination in the workplace, has failed; for proof, proponents point out that for every dollar men earn, women earn just 77 cents.

But that wage gap isn't necessarily the result of discrimination. On the contrary, there are lots of other reasons men might earn more than women, including differences in education, experience and job tenure.

When these factors are taken into account the gap narrows considerably—in some studies, to the point of vanishing. A recent survey found that young, childless, single urban women earn 8 percent more than their male counterparts, mostly because more of them earn college degrees.

[T]here are lots of other reasons men might earn more than women, including differences in education, experience and job tenure.

How Choices Affect Wages

Moreover, a 2009 analysis of wage-gap studies commissioned by the Labor Department evaluated more than 50 peer-reviewed papers and concluded that the aggregate wage gap "may be almost entirely the result of the individual choices being made by both male and female workers."

In addition to differences in education and training, the review found that women are more likely than men to leave the workforce to take care of children or older parents. They also tend to value family-friendly workplace policies more than men, and will often accept lower salaries in exchange for more benefits. In fact, there were so many differences in pay-related choices that the researchers were unable to specify a residual effect due to discrimination.

Some of the bill's supporters admit that the pay gap is largely explained by women's choices, but they argue that those choices are skewed by sexist stereotypes and social pressures. Those are interesting and important points, worthy of continued public debate.

> [Women] also tend to value family-friendly workplace policies more than men, and will often accept lower salaries in exchange for more benefits.

The problem is that while the debate proceeds, the bill assumes the answer: it would hold employers liable for the "lingering effects of past discrimination"—"pay disparities" that have been "spread and perpetuated through commerce." Under the bill, it's not enough for an employer to guard against intentional discrimination; it also has to police potentially discriminatory assumptions behind market-driven wage disparities that have nothing to do with sexism.

Universities, for example, typically pay professors in their business schools more than they pay those in the school of social work, citing market forces as the justification. But according to the gender theory that informs this bill, sexist attitudes led society to place a higher value on male-centered fields like business than on female-centered fields like social work.

The Paycheck Fairness Act Is Unfair to Employers

The bill's language regarding these "lingering effects" is vague, but that's the problem: it could prove a legal nightmare for even the best-intentioned employers. The theory will be elaborated in feminist expert testimony when cases go to trial, and it's not hard to imagine a media firestorm developing from it. Faced with multimillion-dollar lawsuits and the attendant publicity, many innocent employers would choose to settle.

The Paycheck Fairness bill would set women against men, empower trial lawyers and activists, perpetuate falsehoods about the status of women in the workplace and create havoc in a precarious job market. It is 1970s-style gender-war feminism for a society that should be celebrating its success in substantially, if not yet completely, overcoming sex-based workplace discrimination.

7

Money Is Not More Important for Men than Women

Soraya Chemaly

Soraya Chemaly is a feminist, satirist, and media critic. Her writing has appeared at media outlets including the Huffington Post *and the* Feminist Wire.

> *Wage inequality between men and women in the United States continues to exist and is based on longstanding stereotypes and discrimination. Explaining the wage gap as the result of choices women make is unfair: Women are constrained by the social and cultural framework surrounding childrearing and work/family responsibilities. Money is just as important to women as it is to men. Legislation that supports pay equity and family-friendly policies that benefit both women and men are needed to correct the imbalance.*

According to the World Economic Forum's 2011 Global Gender Gap Study, the U.S. ranks 68th in an evaluation of wage equality between men and women among 135 countries that represent 90% of the world's population. Is it "arguable" that earning a living is more important for men than for women, as a Wisconsin state senator suggested earlier this week? Men out-earn women in the U.S. and people in this country think they should continue to do so. Which means individual women, their families and our entire society will continue to pay high prices for what is essentially a broad application of outdated gender stereotypes to economic policy. But hey, the U.S. ranks No. 1 in Miss Universe wins. That's a major relief, because, after all, when women have a vicarious relationship to their income and long term financial security, the currency of their worth is attractiveness, so at least we look good.

Women have made important and major strides in opportunity, work force engagement and pay in the past half century, but next week's April 17 [2012] Equal Pay Day exists for an enduring and legitimate reason. This day symbolically marks how far into the year a woman has to work to make what a man made during the prior calendar year. Yup. That means Jane has to keep working through January, February, March and half of April 2012 in order to bring home the same paycheck that John did in calendar year 2011. Since the Equal Pay Act of 1963, the gap between men's and women's pay (calculated for full-time work) has closed at less than half-a-cent per year. At this rate, we will be "celebrating" this event for fifty more years before the gap closes.

Since the Equal Pay Act of 1963, the gap between men's and women's pay (calculated for full-time work) has closed at less than half-a-cent per year.

You've heard the statistics: The median annual earnings for working (full-time) white women is 77 cents to a man's dollar. For women of color, the gap and its effects are even greater: African-American women earn 61 cents to the male dollar and Latina women earn 53 cents. Controlling for factors like education, experience, job type and more reveals that fully one-quarter to one-half of the gap is attributable to unexplained causes. Women now make up more than half of the U.S. workforce—this gap affects hundreds of millions of people and families.

Why do we have such an intractable gender pay gap, what do these numbers actually mean and how are you personally affected by it?

Longstanding Sexism and Stereotypes

Let me say there are no cabals of mean men, dressed for Scottish Rites, plotting to pay women less. It's a matter of deep cultural habits and systematized sexism borne of dated stereotypes. Unless you live in Wisconsin. In which case, I'm so sorry. Wisconsin is where, while everyone was busy over the weekend, Governor Scott Walker signed a bill repealing the 2009 Equal Pay Enforcement Act which made it easier for victims of pay discrimination to pursue legal redress. Republican state senator Glenn Grothman, a major champion of the charge to repeal the Act, explained to Daily Beast reporter Michelle Goldberg, "You could argue that money is more important for men."

Uh. Wrong. You could argue NOT and accurately reflect the reality of contemporary life. The most recent Department of Labor Statistics reveal that 40% of wives earn more than their husbands and, according to recent Pew Research studies, women are increasingly earning heads of household (22%). Lastly, due to divorce, widowhood or no marriage, more than half of children born to women under 30 have single, sole-breadwinning mothers. If the wage gap didn't exist, the poverty rate for single mothers would be half of what it is. Boys and men might still feeling a sluggish but strong pressure to provide for dependent women and children. And there are women who feel they are right in doing so. But, we are so far past the days when *most* women can either afford to or want to have a vicarious and precarious relationship with their income. Women need to be able to earn their own money *while* raising children. True "family values" would reflect an investment of time, money and political capital to helping them to this without either short-term income or long term security penalization.

Forget, for just a moment, debates about the inputs and analysis that produce these numbers year after year, and consider this: What do those numbers mean in terms of lost wages and spending power?

If the wage gap didn't exist, the poverty rate for single mothers would be half of what it is.

According to economists at The Wage Project, over the course of her lifetime a woman will earn, on average, this much less for her work than a man of comparable education: If she has a high school degree she will earn $700K less; a college degree, $1.2 million less and, gosh, if she has a professional degree that number is in excess of $1.8 million. Unless she's in Virginia, there she will lose more than $2,000,000 over the course of her working life. What if this gap didn't exist for women in Virginia? How much more could a woman afford during the course of a year?

- For starters, 1.8 years' worth or 95 more weeks of food

- Half a year's worth of utilities and mortgage payments

- More than 3,000 gallons of gasoline

- Eleven extra months of rent

- Oh, and, I almost forgot—nearly three additional years of health insurance premiums for her family.

In addition, consider the ramifications of the lifetime wage gap in terms women's ability to:

- Save for retirement

- Accrue Social Security benefits

- Rely on pension plans and

- Save for lifetime goals (like buying a house). . . .

The broad impact on our economy is immeasurable loss. As succinctly articulated by Gloria Feldt, author of *No Excuses: 9 Ways Women Can Change How We Think About Power*: "For a thriving 21st century economy, America can't afford to lose half its population's contributions."

Mr. Grothman and Mr. Walker, like so many of their peers, are nostalgic for a bygone era based on the outdated and onerous-for-all idea of all-male, sole-breadwinner responsibility. Grothman continued: "I think a guy in their first job (sic), maybe because they expect to be a breadwinner someday, may be a little more money-conscious. To attribute everything to a so-called bias in the workplace is just not true." Personally, I'd rather attribute it to ignorance, paternalistic sexism and a blithe denial of modern economies. But, to be fair, I imagine that Mr. Grothman is simply trying to help sex-seeking young guys by making sure they have a "dining budget" to go a-courtin'. Pat Robertson captured the essence of this "man-up" approach to finances this weekend when he instructed Evangelical faithful men to "push forward and your wife will come along." I know, I know, some people don't want to get too feminist-thinky about money and sex and get befuddled by new-fangled ideas of equality and fairness.

Here's an incontrovertible fact: Regardless of education, experience in the workforce or child-rearing commitments, the gender pay gap remains a stubborn legitimate problem for American women and families (including men, if you can imagine). The effect is magnified for women of color who bear the brunt of the feminization of poverty. Passing legislation that hinders people's ability to seek justice, as Wisconsin just did or as Republican's in Congress have, denies and perpetuates a real problem with real day to day ramifications for people.

There are several dimensions to pay discrimination and a wage gap, many of them wielded as a defensive weapon to explain that the gap is due to women making "choices" that result in lower pay. The choices that women and their families make are a) rational, given the continued imbalanced dynamics of work/family responsibilities and b) false "choices" since both men and women are socially and culturally constrained and unable to consider equally competing and comparable options. Even after taking into account the issue of "choice" gender discrimination remains a marked component of the wage gap measurements.

> "The gender pay gap is a product of the choices people think women and men should make, as well as the choices that they actually make," explains Catherine Hill, Director of Research for the American Association of University Women. "Women's work has long been undervalued, and traditionally female jobs continue to pay less than traditionally male jobs. The fact that women working full-time earn just 77 percent of their male peers shows us the scale of the problem."

The way women with children are treated in the workplace is anachronistic. We penalize women and reward men when children enter the picture.

Reasons for the Gap

Here are the major contributors informing the stats and the debate over their relevance:

1) The Maternal Wage Tax:

The way women with children are treated in the workplace is anachronistic. We penalize women and reward men when children enter the picture. The most minimal "real" pay discrimination period in a woman's life takes place when she is unmarried with no children, college educated in her twenties. In her book, *The Richer Sex*, reporter Lisa Mundy talks about this and predicts that we are on the verge of a "big flip" when women will out-earn men. But, despite the claim of her title, women are not richer and once children enter the picture, the erosion of wages continues to be substantial.

Motherhood is the prime "women make choices" time. Women often work in lower paying sectors, work (outside of the home, for pay) fewer hours a week and therefore fewer paid hours a year than men. They are less likely to get hired (according to The Motherhood Manifesto, 44% less likely) and when they are hired are paid on average 11% less than a childless woman. Their work life is also more likely than men's to be interrupted. Numbers from the Bureau of Labor Statistics show the degree to which the idea that women stop working to care for children (thereby making choices that reduce their pay) is a matter of stereotyping and perception, not reality: 60 percent of women with children under the age of three and 77 percent of mothers with school-age children remain in the workforce. Secondly, these facts ignore the catch-22 that women and their families face due to the cost of working being higher than the gains. We generally still struggle to have family-friendly work cultures that create a more gender equitable work life playing field. This complicated fact is potentially the most important contributor to the gap's perseverance. Most men I know do not ever seriously consider paternity leave—the long-term costs to their careers is too significant. Well, what do you think the long-term cost to a woman's career is? Equally significant. But more women make these "choices" than men do and as long as this gap exists the rational choice will be for the higher income earning partner to stay employed and the lower earning partner to stay at home. Gee, couldn't be because of laws that perpetuate unfair pay practices and enable family-hostile work environments? Or the cultural messages we send children about sex roles, could it?

Quoting Dr. Shelley Correll, who has studied the maternal wage gap for years, MomsRising put it this way:

"We expected to find that moms were going to be discriminated against, but I was surprised by the magnitude of the gap," comments Dr. Correll. "I expected small numbers but we found huge numbers. Another thing was that fathers were actually advantaged and we didn't expect fathers to be offered more money or to be rated higher." But that's what happened. A study by Jane Waldfogel of Columbia University, published in the *Journal of Economic Perspectives*, found the same thing: Men don't take wage hits after having children, women do."

2) A persistently gender segregated work force

Women continue to make up the majority of low-wage earners in jobs such as teaching, administrative support and nursing. They also are more likely to be employed in the public sector, where wages are significantly lower than in the private sector. The number one job held by women in 2010: secretary. Why do women cluster in the lowest paying jobs? Is it a chicken or egg problem? First, many originated as extensions of "nurturing," "mothering" roles and "naturally" women want to do those out of the goodness of their little, womanly hearts. Second, these jobs are perceived as unskilled to some degree— not needing either additional training or graduate degrees. Women chose these jobs for lots of reasons among them are that a) they are "traditional" women's jobs, b) people believe they are more "flexible" which is questionable at best, c) they do not require an investment in higher education, d) women are less likely to pursue traditionally "male" jobs—which often require early childhood educational focus in the sciences and math (that's a whole other issue).

3) Women get a lower return on educational investment in terms of pay

Most people pursue education to improve their lot in life and earn more money. With each level of education, potential earning power increases, as does the lifetime value of an investment in education. Over the course of a man's life, he will make 84% more if he gets a Bachelor's degree than if he stops at high school. There is a correlating jump if he gets a professional degree. For him, each educational step yields a correlating increase in earnings. That's not true for women compared to men. So, whereas women with degrees make more than women without, they still make less than men with the same educational background. Because of wage discrimination, for a woman to make what a man with a high school degree makes, she has to get a college degree. This is true at every level of change in education. Georgetown University's College Payoff study, has details if you care to read more. Multiple studies have consistently found that women earn less than men with similar degrees in the same occupational categories—for full-time work with the same level of experience. Women pursuing higher education do tend to study fields with lower earning potential however, so more English majors, less engineering. But there is an interesting problem with women seeking to diversify their educational and professional options: When women enter traditionally "male" fields they don't earn more money, but instead, salaries and prestige go down.

4) Last but not least, plain old-fashioned sex discrimination

---

[F]or a woman to make what a man with a high school degree makes, she has to get a college degree.

Many people refuse to believe that gender discrimination still exists. In addition to the issues above, debunking myths abound. The US Census American Factfinder reveals apples to apples, full-time pay inequities between women and men doing the same job. For example, women physicians and surgeons earned $120,971, compared with $190,726 for men and women securities, commodities and financial services sales agents earned $52,524, compared to $85,760 for their male counterparts. Multiple studies like the AAUW's 2012 The

Simple Truth, controlled for factors known to affect earnings such as education and training, parenthood and hours worked, "college-educated women still earn five percent less than men one year out of college and 12 percent less than men 10 years out of college." Fully one quarter of the pay gap is unexplained despite attempts to account for differences. The gap is constant, well and consistently documented. Some people simply refuse to believe this can be the case.

Legislation Is Needed

Taking all of this into account might make it easier to understand why pay equity and its relation to long term wage earning equity goes from being a matter of individual discrimination and legal redress to broad systemized societal bias that need to be addressed through legislation and policy. It's also easier to understand how certain types portray women as gold-digging, dependent parasites, seemingly incapable of managing "their" finances. Imagine if men lived in a system where politicians (84% of whom were women) continuously enacted laws that imperiled their ability to earn a living fairly, increased their chances of poverty and long term insecurity? Imagine if the basis for policy was the idea that men's income would be optimized, ideally, through a relationship with a higher wage earning female? They too might make decisions that are rational, but on the surface seem self-defeating or mercenary.

Both "pay equity" statistics (although usefully illustrative) and the arguments debunking these statistics (such as Mr. Grothman's "suggestion" that it is more important for men to make money than for women) are distracting and misleading for three reasons: 1) both strongly suggest an incorrect zero-sum, either/or, women v. men framework for the issue. Valuing women's work and paying them fairly does not penalize men who by and large have to work in economic partnership with women now 2) the focus on "pay" instead of aggregated wages minimizes the issue of women's long-term financial vulnerability and impoverishment which have serious implications for society and 3) emphasizing "pay" obscures our country's lack of policy commitment to family friendly policies, maternal and paternal leave and other structures that support working mothers (and fathers) instead of penalizing them.

Imagine if men lived in a system where politicians (84% of whom were women) continuously enacted laws that imperiled their ability to earn a living fairly . . . ?

There are several ways to address these issues and they are all necessary. One is for companies to understand the value of family friendly policies from which men and women can both benefit. Many already pursue these policies to positive effect, but they are the minority. Lists of which companies are ranked for best work life balance benefits abound. Those that focus on the best companies for working mothers also tend to be the best for working fathers. The second is to make sure that legislation related to fair pay is not revoked or is passed when up for a vote. The Paycheck Fairness Act, which is vital to addressing this gap and eliminating loopholes, is up for a vote in Congress and may not pass. In an effort to stem the tide of women to the Democratic party, Republican candidates are now using words like "kitchen table" decisions. The problem is, deep down they still think the only people at the kitchen table are women and that they are making their decisions when their husbands come home after a long day at work. . . .

8

Unions Help Women's Wages

Sarah Standiford

Sarah Standiford is executive director of the Maine Women's Lobby, a nonpartisan advocacy group.

The gender wage gap is persistent and devastating to women and families. Legislation that promotes fair pay must be protected and promoted. The Paycheck Fairness Act is one way to address wage discrimination. Another important measure is to keep unions strong. Unions can benefit women as much as a college education when it comes to workplace safety, security, and wage fairness.

For women across the country, today [April 12, 2011] is an important day—the nationwide observance of Equal Pay Day. The date symbolizes how far into 2011 women must work to earn what men earned in 2010.

According to the most recent U.S. Census Bureau statistics, women who work in full-time, year-round jobs in Maine earn, on average, 76.7 cents for every dollar earned by men working in those jobs.

The persistent gender wage gap is more than simply a matter of fairness. Maine's wage gap leaves women and their families shortchanged by thousands of dollars a year—and hundreds of thousands of dollars over the course of a lifetime.

Pay Inequality Affects Everyone

The wage gap not only depresses women's incomes over the short term, but also weakens retirement security down the road. In some cases, it keeps women—and the families they support—poor.

So what can we do to address the inequity? The Paycheck Fairness Act, which failed to pass the U.S. Senate last year [2010] on a close procedural vote (despite the support of a majority of senators), would help. The bill is an update to the nation's 48-year-old fair pay laws.

Paycheck Fairness would strengthen incentives for preventing wage discrimination and prohibit retaliation against workers who inquire about employers' wage practices. It's due to be reintroduced in the 112th Congress this week [March, 2012].

In the previous Congress, Paycheck Fairness was championed by Maine's two Democrats in the House, Reps. Mike Michaud and Chellie Pingree. This time around, it deserves the support of Maine's entire delegation.

Here's an even simpler way to promote fair pay: Keep Maine's existing protections on the books.

Stop Legislation That Weakens Unions

The fact is, several bills in the state Legislature would make access to fair pay all the more difficult for women, and would erase the gains women have already made in the work force.

For example, Gov. Paul Le-Page is promoting legislation to undermine unions—part of an effort to weaken Maine's worker protections, such as child labor and overtime laws.

This is a problem because, simply put, unions are one of the very best ways for women to achieve paycheck fairness. So-called "right to work" bills are part of a national effort that included the drive to weaken workers' collective bargaining rights in Wisconsin.

The bills, if enacted, would stop employers and employees from negotiating an agreement—also known as a union security clause—that says that all workers who receive the benefits of a collective bargaining agreement share the costs of representation.

"Right to work" laws make it illegal for unions to collect fees for services that the law requires them to provide. The result is clear: weaker unions with fewer resources to defend the workers they represent.

If we allow our unions to be undercut, women's earnings will suffer.

That's why workers in states with these misnamed laws make less money and have fewer benefits. In fact, all people in "right to work" states have a lower standard of living—lower wages, higher poverty rates, less access to health care, less safe workplaces.

Research Shows Women Benefit from Unions

If we allow our unions to be undercut, women's earnings will suffer. For women, the union advantage has always been evident. Findings from the Center for Economic Policy and Research, which analyzed data from the U.S. Census Bureau's Current Population Survey, found that unionization raises the pay of women workers by almost $2 per hour.

Says economist John Schmitt, author of the 2008 report: "For women, joining a union makes as much sense as going to college. All else equal, joining a union raises a woman's wage as much as a full year of college, and a union raises the chances a woman has health insurance by more than earning a four-year college degree."

There are two proven ways for women to increase their earnings. One is access to higher education. After all, the gender wage gap means that a typical woman needs to have a bachelor's degree in order to make the same amount that a male high school graduate earns.

The second way is to be part of a collective bargaining agreement, which levels the playing field for everyone.

If Mainers allow these "right to work" bills to pass in the Legislature this year, Maine women will pay the higher price.

9

Unions Hurt Women's Opportunities

Carrie Lukas

Carrie Lukas is the executive director of the Independent Women's Forum.

Unions have a negative effect on businesses and the economy while only benefiting certain workers. Unions work by regulating workers' pay but also by regulating their time and flexibility, the latter two being particularly important job aspects for female workers. In addition, unions are often corrupt and locked into unhealthy relationships with political leaders.

Unions are supposed to represent workers' interests. Yet while unions increase compensation for their members, they create a less dynamic economy—and as such, increasingly fail to meet the true, long-term interests of workers. In particular, women pay a high price for this intervention.

While union workers on average receive higher pay than non-union workers, only some workers gain during this process—not all. For example, those (disproportionately female) workers who prefer less traditional work arrangements and would trade higher pay for more flexibility lose in union-created one-size-fits-all compensation regimes.

Unions Are Bad for Business

Unions' higher wages also create costs for the companies and consumers. Companies raise prices to compensate for higher employment costs. Unions make companies less competitive, which is why some union shops struggle to survive (and need taxpayer-financed bailouts to avoid bankruptcy). When businesses flounder, employees lose jobs.

In addition, the government's relationship with unions also takes a toll on the economy. Political corruption is inherent in these relationships, creating an unlevel playing field for non-union workers and a less dynamic economy.

At present, the federal government is advancing policies to encourage greater unionization. This is the wrong direction. A dynamic economy, in which new companies are created and existing firms expand, is the most important way to ensure workers have the variety of job opportunities that they want and need. . . .

Ideology Versus Reality

People like to think of unions as protecting workers from big businesses that might otherwise take advantage of employees. In the private sector, employers want to minimize compensation costs to make businesses more profitable and competitive. Unions enable workers to join together to secure fair compensation and safe working conditions from powerful employers.

That's how it's supposed to work, anyway!

However, today unions play an increasingly destructive role in our economy. Unions have become largely a political force, working with politicians (who they support with generous campaign contributions) to create rules that favor union workers and funnel taxpayer resources into union pockets.

In many cases, unions succeed in negotiating more generous benefit packages for members than the average non-union worker receives. However, these benefits come with high costs for the economy, consumers, taxpayers, and ultimately, often for workers themselves.

Who Are Union Workers Today?

When most Americans hear the term "union workers," they think of men working on production lines or in dangerous coal mines. Yet that's not an accurate picture of unions today.

According to the Bureau of Labor Statistics (BLS), less than 12 percent of American workers now belong to a union—down from more than 20 percent in 1983. As of 2010, there were 14.7 million wage and salary union workers. More than half of them (7.6 million) don't work for a company at all, but are government employees. That means that instead of negotiating with company executives, they negotiate with politicians (whose primary interest is to stay in power) in order to expand the size and scope of government, and thus, to increase the need for more unionized government employees.

[N]ot all union workers are necessarily better off as a result of unionization.

Unions Only Help Certain Workers

BLS data shows that among full-time wage and salary workers, union members' median earnings are 28 percent higher than non-union workers. Other studies that control for factors such as age, sex, education, and industry, find similar effects, with union workers earning between 15 and 25 percent more than similarly situated non-union workers.

However, while it's clear that unions benefit some workers, not all union workers are necessarily better off as a result of unionization. Union contracts tend to make it hard to fire or demote less productive workers. This may help some workers who might have otherwise lost their jobs. But it may also discourage companies from taking a chance on lower-skilled workers, with companies instead hiring fewer, more productive workers. That's bad news for workers who need entry-level jobs.

Similarly, unionized pay schedules may benefit average employees, but by preventing companies from rewarding the best performers, some highly productive employees may be made worse off by their union contract.

Union Rules Can Hurt Female Workers

Women are more likely than men to seek out part-time positions or non-traditional work relationships. Unionized contracts therefore can act as an impediment to giving women the flexible work opportunities they need.

For women who are already employed in union shops, this may mean that they simply have less freedom to create schedules that make sense for them. Those who would gladly trade higher pay for reduced hours may find that's impossible due to union rules. Women who aren't currently employed, but who are seeking part-time opportunities are likely to find that difficult in many union shops.

Union protocols can also deter women from entering or switching professions. As the Heritage Institute's James Sherk puts it, "unions function as labor cartels." They restrict the number of workers that an institution can employ, driving up wages for those in the limited labor pool. That's nice for those receiving higher wages, but bad news for those with fewer opportunities to work.

Those who would gladly trade higher pay for reduced hours may find that's impossible due to union rules.

In highly unionized industries, like teaching, this means keeping many qualified women (or men) out of the job market. Across the country, union-negotiated rules tend to make it difficult (if not impossible) for school districts to hire the PhD math whiz that has been a stay-at-home mom but who now wants to teach part-time. Rules about certification and seniority benefit union members at the expense of other potential workers and students who would benefit from a more diverse, higher quality teaching force.

Political Corruption

Increasingly, the most important dynamic in determining what union workers make isn't the balance between the union and companies. It's between *politicians* and unions.

As noted previously, today, most union workers get their paychecks from taxpayers. That means that politicians and government bureaucrats negotiate deals with government unions and decide how much union workers are paid and what benefits they receive.

These politicians' primary interest isn't the profitability of any enterprise or even making the most efficient use of their resources. Typically, they're focused on staying in power.

Ideally, that would mean providing citizens with efficient, effective services. But often it means pleasing the unions themselves. Unions are very politically active, donating millions and providing legions of volunteers to work on campaigns and at polls for politicians "friendly" to government-union interests. . . .

The Best Worker Protection: A Dynamic, Growing Economy

The United States faces a serious jobs crisis. Our official unemployment rate is 9.1 percent, but if we were to include discouraged and under-employed workers, a far higher number (16.2 percent of Americans) are facing hardship.

One reason why our economy is struggling is that it lacks flexibility, and too many of our national resources are being used to defend inefficient industries and jobs. Unions make this problem worse. Wasteful government spending increases the tax burden on America's private sector workers and adds to our ballooning government debt. Subsidizing union companies unfairly disadvantages non-union firms, discourages the creation of new start-ups, leads to higher prices for goods and services, and makes our economy less dynamic and innovative.

We all want workers to have good wages, benefits, and the flexibility to work in positions that meet their unique needs. Policymakers can best pursue that goal by returning power and resources to the private sector so that companies and individuals can channel resources to where they will be put to best use. That will lead to more innovation, more start-ups, and a more dynamic, flexible economy that will create job opportunities for all . . . .

10

Women's Lower Wages Are Compounded by Dwindling Social Services

Rosa DeLauro and Heidi Hartmann

Rosa DeLauro is a congresswoman who represents the 3rd District of Connecticut. Heidi Hartman is president of the Institute for Women's Policy Research.

States' budgetary woes have led to two issues that put a disproportionate burden on women. Anti-union efforts are threatening state and local public sector jobs, the majority of which are held by women. Budget cuts are decimating public services, the majority of which are also used by women. The compounding effect of these two phenomena makes it an important time to stand up for women's workplace issues.

Across America, hardworking teachers, police officers, fire-fighters, nurses and other public employees are being squeezed from two directions.

On one hand, cutting deficits has become the main budgetary priority in Washington and state capitals, which means pay freezes or layoffs for hundreds of thousands of these middle-class workers. Meanwhile, in Wisconsin, Ohio, Indiana and other states, governors are using the real problem of budget deficits as a justification to pursue a long-term goal: union busting.

Whether by design or default, this two-pronged assault on the public sector disproportionately hurts women.

Over the course of a career, women lose out on anywhere from $400,000 to $2 million in earnings—simply for being female.

Women in the Public Sector

Women are the majority of public-sector employees at the state and local levels and have already lost 320,000 public-sector jobs in the past two years. As budget crises intensify this year [2011], and as states still face a $125 billion budget shortfall, state governments are likely to shed more jobs. These layoffs are likely to fall squarely on women.

Worse, job losses will come as female workers are trying to do more with less because they have already begun in the hole. College-educated public servants, for example, make 32 percent less than their private-sector counterparts. Because of pay discrimination, women make 77 cents on the dollar compared with men. Over the course of a career, women lose out on anywhere from $400,000 to $2 million in earnings—simply for being female. As a result, 28 percent of unmarried working women with children live below the poverty line, compared with 6 percent of working men.

Women and Social Services

Similarly, women not only are the majority of public-sector workers, they more often need government services. Women are 60 percent of those receiving the earned income and child tax credits, which serve mainly working parents. And women are more than two-thirds of those receiving food stamps.

Just as government is rolling back its commitment to these programs, the number of families that need this help is greater than ever.

To complicate matters, the new House Republican majority is trying to drastically cut education, job training and health care services. For example, the Head Start early-education program faces a $1 billion cut—meaning 55,000 teachers and aides would be laid off. K-12 education is predicted to see a cut of almost $600 million. That means approximately 17,000 teacher layoffs. Job training programs would be eliminated with a cut of more than $4 billion to the work force investment system.

In addition, the GOP [Grand Old Party] majority is attempting to defund Title X services, which have connected millions of American women to health care since 1970. Republicans want to repeal the Affordable Health Care Act, which ended the pernicious practice of gender rating—charging women more for the same coverage—and at long last put women's health care on an equal footing.

Equal pay for equal work will reduce the burden on the safety net. . . .

How Can We Protect Women?

The danger to American women in these rollbacks is clear. The question is: What do we do about it? How do we turn back these assaults on women at all levels of government?

First, we can call out the anti-union tactics for what they are. Some governors are attempting to use the state budget crises as a pretense to fulfill a long-term ideological agenda and scale back the provision of public services. By eliminating collective-bargaining rights for public-sector workers, the U.S. loses its strongest champions of critical government services.

If residents can no longer count on government for education, public safety or even roads, they will have to fend for themselves. Under a privatized scenario, those with higher incomes will be the only ones who can afford these services. Average working women and men will be left out and the middle-class standard of living will decline.

Second, we should support strong investments in education, job training and health care. The future of America depends on not turning back the clock on these critical work force investments.

Businesses are looking for the employees who can make them successful. Because the federal government is the only institution that can backstop revenue losses at other levels of government, it falls to Congress to make these critical investments when states and localities are feeling the pinch.

Legislation That Helps Women

Third, we should pass the Paycheck Fairness Act, which will give teeth to the Equal Pay Act, bringing sex discrimination law into parity with all other types of discriminatory law—giving female workers the tools to ensure they are fairly compensated. Equal pay for equal work will reduce the burden on the safety net—and thus reduce deficits.

What is at stake in Wisconsin, Ohio, Indiana and other states is more than a budget crisis. It is whether we as a nation will stand up for the rights of working middle-class women and men to improve their lives or make it harder for them and their families to seize opportunities—at home or at work, in college or in our hospitals.

If this assault on public-sector unions succeeds, Americans may lose not only their bargaining rights in the workplace but the critical services they rely on.

We can and must do better.

11

Women Executives Earn Less than Their Male Counterparts

Jena McGregor

Former management editor at Businessweek, *Jena McGregor is the author of the* Washington Post's *blog "On Leadership."*

According to a recent survey by the Corporate Library, even CEOs are not immune to the male-female wage gap. While women tend to earn a higher base salary, their overall compensation is significantly lower. Possible explanations include shortened tenure for women, lack of women's risk-taking in negotiations, and a double standard in how women's performance is evaluated.

The gender pay gap is a well established phenomenon: Women who work full time made about 79% as much as full-time male workers in 2007. While the number has narrowed slightly over the decades, it's an unfortunate, if persistent, fact in workforce economics. The explanations are varied and complex: Women are more likely to leave the workforce for a few years to care for family, sadly don't do as much negotiating for their pay, and in some industries, don't always pursue the highest paying roles. And undoubtedly, discrimination still plays a role in some cases.

That said, one place you wouldn't think a gap would still exist is among CEOs, where pay for performance should eliminate any such bias. But alas, The Corporate Library, a corporate governance research firm, is out with a study today saying that indeed, total compensation for women CEOs lags behind male CEOs after all. According to the latest findings from "The Corporate Library's CEO Pay Survey: CEO Pay 2008," female CEO pay packages are only about 85% of male total actual pay (which includes stock option profits and other realized equity) at the median: $1,746,000 compared to $2,049,000. The survey adjusted for size, industry, tenure and performance and included 3,242 U.S. and Canadian-based companies.

The gap is the widest for female CEOs of the largest companies, who make less than two thirds of their male counterparts.

Female CEOs Get Higher Base Salaries

Interestingly, the study finds that female chiefs get higher base salaries—103% of median male salaries. But add in cash bonuses, perks and stock compensation—the goodies that really get CEO pay skyrocketing—and the differential is clear. The gap is the widest for female CEOs of the largest companies, who make less than two thirds of their male counterparts.

The study's authors attempt to explain the differential, but don't have an easy time. They question whether industry could perhaps play a role: More than 15 percent of women CEOs lead financial services companies, where performance has been pummeled, hurting pay packages, compared to 12 percent of male CEOs. Still, they say, the distribution was not different enough to have a significant or consistent effect. Performance wasn't enough, either. While relative total shareholder returns by female-led companies "showed a higher proportion underperforming the index than male-led companies" in the shorter term, the difference narrowed over longer-term periods.

Tenure, they concluded, could have some impact on long-term equity payments, as women CEOs have slightly shorter median tenures than men. But in the end, the cause may be a result of the greater problem. "Perhaps it is the number of female CEOs," speculated Senior Research Associate Paul Hodgson, one of the report's co-authors. "Less than 3 percent of CEOs were women, so there were nearly 33 times as many male CEOs as there were female CEOs. This is a shockingly low number in any major Western economy, but the small number of women in the sample—only 80—may be affecting the findings."

Undervalued by Themselves and Others

I'd add a couple others, based on a story I wrote a few months ago on some research by a group of researchers at Britain's University of Exeter and Tilburg University in the Netherlands. They studied bonuses paid to 96 pairs of executive-level men and women in Britain with similar experience. Women, they found, were rewarded less for improved results. They attributed the difference, for one, to women's risk-taking in negotiating pay packages.

In addition, they believe the difference is due to the unfortunate, but apparently greater, likelihood that leadership success is ascribed to male leaders. "A lot of research shows [men receive] a lot of internal attributions—people think that he must be responsible for increasing or decreasing" performance, says one of the study authors, Clara Kulich. "With a female manager, [boards are] more prone to use external situations, economic situations," she says, noting almost an "indifference" to the women leader's impact.

12

Women CEOs May Outearn Male Counterparts in Some Areas

Bianna Golodryga and Michael Murray

Bianna Golodryga is co-anchor of Good Morning America's *weekend edition and a business correspondent for ABC News. Michael Murray is a contributing writer to this article.*

An elite group of female CEOs are bucking the male-female wage gap. The public nature of CEO salaries may be one explanation. It's unclear whether these highly paid women can influence—from the top down—the pay gap that still affects the vast majority of working women.

While the average earnings for women still lag behind those of men, they're turning the tables in the most exclusive corporate club of all. A new report from Bloomberg News, the leading provider of business news worldwide, shows that women who head the nation's largest companies are earning substantially more than their male counterparts. Their average annual pay over the last few years? Just over $14 million dollars.

"That means women earned 40 percent more than men in 2009," says Alexis Leondis of Bloomberg.

[In] 2009 female CEOs got raises averaging nearly 30 percent, while male CEOs took pay cuts.

Sixteen Women at the Top

Carol Bartz, the CEO of Yahoo! has a pay package of $47.2 million.

Kraft CEO Irene Rosenfeld's take-home pay is $26.3 million.

And Indra Nooyi, the CEO of Pepsi Co., earns $15.8 million a year.

Despite those huge salaries, there is a huge caveat: There are still very few women who have made it to the corner office when compared to the number of men in those positions of corporate power. Only 16 companies listed in the S&P 500 are run by women.

One reason female bosses did so much better than women at lower levels is that CEO pay is transparent, being made public and available to the press. Some say no board would dare underpay a female CEO for fear of public backlash.

[In] 2009 female CEOs got raises averaging nearly 30 percent, while male CEOs took pay cuts.

"There's 16 women making money and that's great," says Marie Wilson of The White House Project, a women's advocacy group. "I'm concerned about the vast majority of women who are now the majority of the workforce . . . it's kind of like the 16 supercorporate women are doing well. And that's a good sign—but it's not good enough."

In fact, women workers as a whole earn just 79% as much as men, according to the U.S. Bureau of Labor Statistics.

So Why Do Most Women Struggle?

Although these 16 women CEOs have climbed to the top rung of the corporate ladder, most women still struggle to get a solid foothold. Some studies have shown that women are far less aggressive in negotiations.

In one ABC News behavior lab experiment, volunteers were told they would be paid between $5 and $12 for their time participating in a study. Everyone was offered the minimum, but the men and women differed wildly in their reactions to the payment. More than half the men asked for more money, but only a third of the women bargained for more.

Women CEOs Earn More, But Not Their Assistants

But still, even the women who have broken through the glass ceiling say that much has to change culturally in the business for women to reach parity at all levels. The hope is that the few who have made it to the top can start that change from the highest levels.

"If my job went out there with that kind of earning, I guess I'd want to make a real commitment to seeing every woman in my company paid fairly," says Wilson. "If I'm being paid like that I want all of you to be paid fairly."

13

CEOs with Daughters Pay Women More

Kimberly Weisul

Kimberly Weisul is the previous senior editor of Businessweek.

The gender wage gap is present worldwide. However, a recent study in Denmark found that male CEOs begin to close the pay gap of their employees after having a daughter. The effect was most pronounced when the daughter was their first born. Pay was raised more for women with more education.

Is your CEO about to become a father? If you're a woman employee at his company, you should hope the newborn is a girl.

Professors Michael Dahl of Aalborg University in Denmark, Cristian Dezsö of the University of Marylan's Robert H. Smith School of Business, and David Gaddis Ross at Columbia Business School recently completed a study of the gender pay gap in the Danish workplace.

Worldwide, women earn an estimated 9 to 18 percent less than men with the same job descriptions and equivalent education and experience. Denmark, despite being considered a relatively egalitarian society, still has a wage gap. It's also the ideal place to study wage gaps, because the government keeps very thorough demographic statistics on its population and on every Danish company.

CEOs and Daughters

Earlier research suggested that US legislators who have daughters tend to vote more liberally on women's issues, especially issues of reproductive rights. So the researchers thought a male CEO who had a daughter would be more likely to try to narrow the wage gap at his company. "There is something about a female child," says Ross, "that makes these issues more salient to male CEOs."

Earlier research suggested that US legislators who have daughters tend to vote more liberally on women's issues, especially issues of reproductive rights.

Shortly after the CEOs had daughters, the women's wages at their companies began to rise relative to men's, shrinking the wage gap.

First daughters who were also firstborns had the biggest effect. These girls helped close the wage gap at their dads' companies by three percent.

First daughters who were not firstborns still helped narrow the wage gap. At companies headed by their dads, the wage gap closed by 0.8 percent.

Most of the gains in wages were found at smaller firms, or those with 10-50 employees. (Firms with fewer than 10 employees were not included in the study) The researchers believe this is because at smaller companies, CEOs have more influence over the pay of individual employees. The birth of any daughter at these firms shrunk the wage gap by about 1%.

Highly-educated women employees benefited more than others. Since most CEOs are highly educated, it makes sense that they would see well-educated women as potential proxies for their own grown daughters. Among college educated women, the birth of a daughter (firstborn or not) closed the gender gap by about 1%. Do you believe there is a wage gap at your company? If so, how important do you think the CEO's outlook could be in closing it?

14

CEOs with Daughters Will Not Solve the Gender Pay Gap

C.V. Harquail

C.V. Harquail is a leadership and organizational change consultant who writes about aligning organizational identity, action, and purpose at AuthenticOrganizations.com.

The idea that CEO "Daddies of Daughters" will help close the gender wage gap is completely misleading. This idea encourages society to buy into CEO Daddy "Feminism," which is just another way to allow business men (and women) to avoid taking responsibility for gender inequity in the workplace.

When solid but small bits of research get big buzz about nothing actionable, my inner curmudgeon comes out. Given the play that a recent study is getting, all about how having a daughter makes a male CEO deal with the gender wage gap, the curmudgeon must speak:

The unpublished working paper has been blogged, featured on Yahoo news, and discussed in the Wall Street Journal Review Section (the 'thinking' section of the WSJ), all because of this finding:

A new, not-yet-published study that tracked 12 years of wage data in Denmark finds that when male CEOs had daughters, their female employees' wages went up 1.3 percent while their male employees only gained .8 percent raises. So the birth of a daughter effectively shrunk the male-female wage gap by .5 percent on average.

And the takeaway is supposed to be this:

When a daughter is born to a CEO, the male-female wage gap at his company is reduced.

Ergo, having a daughter makes a man more likely to use his professional power to make the world of work a better place for women. *Having a baby girl makes a CEO Daddy a Feminist.*

Interesting spin, isn't it. Let's investigate.

In real dollars, this means that in a company where a man has been paid $100 and a woman has been paid $82, her wages would go up a whopping $2.80.

Does Having a Baby Girl Really Make A Difference? A Real Difference?

Let's look closely at the study itself. The spin starts with the way that the finding is presented. Although the finding is statistically significant, the size of the effect is small. Said another way, the relationship between Daddy CEO having a Girl and reduction in the gender wage gap is not a function of chance. And, it doesn't make much of a real world difference.

On average, the decrease was .5% (yes, half of one percent). In the best case scenario, in a small company (less than 50 employees) where the CEO's *first born* child is a girl, the impact of her birth on that CEO Daddy's actions towards women's pay is very small—a decrease in the wage gap of 2.8%. In real dollars, this means that in a company where a man has been paid $100 and a woman has been paid $82, her wages would go up a whopping $2.80.

Post-daughter, post-CEO Feminist enlightenment, the woman makes *only $15.20 less than the man* who makes $100.

And, if we depend on CEO Daddys, it will take a long time to reach pay equity. To close an 18% wage gap, it would take a company 7 CEOs, (avg. CEO tenure 7 years), each with a first-born daughter, each improving the wage gap by 2.8% per CEO, a full 49 years.

The Research Itself Isn't the Problem

On the plus side, this research does demonstrate empirically that the change in attitudes towards women by new fathers of daughters, already documented in social psychological studies, is likely to exist in the business world as well.

The quality of the data set allowed the researchers to eliminate several kinds of statistical and research design-related challenges to any findings. The assumptions built into their empirical analysis are also quite conservative which increases our confidence that the effect is real.

And, the data are from the real world (not in the laboratory), demonstrating that the effect exists in business settings—in Denmark, anyway.

On the down side, the study offers us no actionable insight. There's not much we can to to increase the number of daughters born to the female partners of male CEOs.

The Real Problem Is the Idea of CEO Daddy Feminism

The real problem with the way this study has been 'spun.' What's been promoted is the idea that having a daughter leads a business man to be less sexist in his business decisions. Somehow, all we need to do is wait for powerful men to have daughters, and sexism at work will get fixed.

But that's not true.

(Certainly some large portion of Fortune 500 (male) CEOs have daughters, but gender wage gaps exist in all of these firms. George Bush had a first-born daughter, and so did Rupert Murdoch. Has either man taken a leadership role for gender equity? No.)

Like the stealth discrimination promoted by so-called 'benevolent sexism,' CEO Daddy Feminism discriminates more than it liberates.

This study is being sold to us so that we'll believe in the idea of CEO Daddy "Feminism"—a special kind of paternalistic (dare I say, patriarchical) form of concern for women. Like the stealth discrimination promoted by so-called 'benevolent sexism,' Daddy Feminism discriminates more than it liberates.

- CEO Daddy Feminism depends on him caring about "his" daughter—rather than asking him to care about everyone's daughters.

- CEO Daddy Feminism depends on him acting paternalistically towards someone beneath him—rather than asking him to address the discrimination that his wife, his sister, his mother, his colleagues, and his age peers have experienced and continue to experience.

- CEO Daddy Feminism depends on him caring about someone he individually identifies with—rather than asking him to be empathic regarding all women.

- CEO Daddy Feminism allows him to wait until he has little to lose—rather than asking him to examine his own privilege in the here and how.

- CEO Daddy Feminism allows him to do only a little bit, for some gains in the long term, rather than to use his power to eliminate gender discrimination at work right now.

The problem of focusing on CEO Daddy Feminism as a possible solution is that it suggests that it's okay only to act on your own child's behalf, and only in small increments that never really effect the CEO himself.

This is not to dismiss the role having a daughter or a son, or a wife or a sister, or a mother or a grandmother can play in bringing a man to become aware of sexism.

Don't read this as a dismissal of the enlightenment, empathy, and action that can come from a man (or woman) finally realizing how sexism and other injustices are hurting people he loves.

And, don't read this as a dismissal of the role that a feminist awakening can play in leading any man (or woman) with power to start to use that power to create equity.

15

Domestic Work and Childrearing Can Be Financially Quantified

Salary.com

Salary.com is a website aimed at helping businesses and individuals manage pay and performance.

Salary.com's annual Mom Salary Survey attempts to put a price tag on the work of motherhood. The final salary combines ten different professions and takes into account variables such as overtime.

Let's get one thing straight right off the bat: moms are priceless. We know this. It doesn't matter if we're talking stay-at-home moms or career moms who seamlessly balance work and family—it's impossible to truly quantify everything mothers do on a daily basis. And because they make it all seem so effortless, it's easy to take their contributions for granted.

That's why every year for the last 12 years, Salary.com has surveyed thousands of mothers across the country to figure out which jobs they spend the most time on and how many hours they work in a week. Then, using our extensive salary data, we figure out how much mothers would earn annually if they were actually paid for the work they do. Is it an exact science? Of course not. But anything that brings to light the hard work of mothers is a good thing.

And this year, as always, moms continue to amaze.

Moms Are Worth More than You Think

We surveyed more than 8,000 moms to find out how much time they spend on their most common tasks. Did you know stay-at-home moms average a 95-hour work week? Or how about working moms, who spend 9 to 5 at the office and then put in an additional 58 hours a week on their household and childcare duties?

Career moms say they are busier than ever, and that's reflected by a 5 percent increase in their "mom salary" compared to last year. Their time spent on "mom jobs" is up an average of two hours a week, which could be a nod to the after effects of the recent recession that had an increased number of women entering the workforce. To that end, stay-at-home mothers saw their "mom salary" drop roughly two percent from 2011, mainly because they reported spending roughly two hours per week less on childcare and household duties.

Stay-at-home moms work a total of 94.7 hours a week, with a 40-hour base and 54.7 hours of overtime on their mom duties.

But no matter your situation, you can go to the Mom Salary Wizard this year, plug in your (or your mom's) info, and print out a fake check for your mom in recognition of how valuable she is to you. And then, make sure you read on to find out more facts about our survey and for the chance to give your mom the Mother's Day present of a lifetime....

Add It All Together and Mothers Are Worth . . .

After averaging the salaries of these top 10 mom jobs, we were able to calculate how much moms would earn if they actually received a paycheck for their work, including overtime pay.

Stay-at-home moms work a total of 94.7 hours a week, with a 40-hour base and 54.7 hours of overtime on their mom duties. That's good for an annual salary of $112,962, or $17.80 an hour. But we all know the value of raising one or more people into quality human beings cannot ever be truly calculated.

Working moms make less with an estimated annual salary of $66,979, logging 57.9 hours a week (40 base, 17.9 of OT), regarding their mom duties. But that doesn't take into account the 35.7 hours a week these career moms are averaging at a paying job, where they make an average annual salary of $45,515. Working mothers have a constant tightrope to walk in balancing family and home, which makes the work they do in both arenas that much more impressive.

But whether they stay at home or work, all moms deserve our respect, love and perpetual gratitude.

16

Women Should Not Be Financially Compensated for Child-Rearing

Ruth Graham

Ruth Graham is a journalist and editor.

The notion of a "mommy" salary, as put forward by South African businesswoman Wendy Luhabe, is nonsensical and misguided. Jobs always include a mix of salary and benefits. Those who choose to be a stay-at-home mom forgo a salary for enormous benefits. It's a personal choice and doesn't require or deserve financial compensation.

In an interview [in April, 2012] with CNN, influential South African businesswoman Wendy Luhabe raises the idea of paying stay at home mothers 10% of their husband's wages as a "mommy salary." The wages would demonstrate that the work of raising children has societal value, and would make the choice to stay home financially viable for more women. "Money is the currency that we use to define value of a contribution to the world," Luhabe says, "so why shouldn't we do the same for the work of bringing up children, which I think is probably the most important contribution that the world should be valuing." That sounds lovely! It's also a terrible idea.

First, an important disclaimer: I agree with Luhabe that mothering is one of the most important jobs in the world.

Staying home full-time to raise children is a personal decision. That choice, and the work that comes with it, should be respected and honored, and in most corners of our culture, it is.

Who Would Pay This "Mommy Salary?"

So, with that out of the way: Luhabe's idea of paying stay-at-home-moms for their work is nonsense. Set aside the fact that she doesn't suggest where exactly this extra money is coming from—the government? the husbands' employer? a money tree and/or fairy?—and consider the impulse behind it.

If women who choose to stay home—who voluntarily opt out of the workforce—should be paid for exercising that choice, then should we all be paid for whatever we choose to do? It calls to mind Lisa Simpson shouting "I choose my choice!" or the classic *Onion* piece titled "Women Now Empowered By Everything A Woman Does." ("According to a study released Monday, women—once empowered primarily via the assertion of reproductive rights or workplace equality with men—are now empowered by virtually everything the typical woman does.")

Maybe someday we'll conjure up some sort of utopian alternate universe in which everyone is handed cash for walking down the street simply because we deserve money for any decision we make.

Money Is Not the Only Reward

The "mommy salary" proposal also validates the notion that money is the only reward worth working for. Traditional jobs come with two forms of compensation: Salary and benefits. If the benefits are great, you might settle for a lower salary. Staying home with children comes with enormous benefits that parents who work full-time in offices forgo. That's part of the deal.

We all make career choices with this balance in mind. Two years ago [in 2010], in a period of personal and professional ennui, I quit my job to take a 10-week road trip by myself all around the United States. It was one of the most important experiences of my life. And of course, I had to give up my salary to do it. It was worth it. It would never occurred to me that someone should be paying me for it simply because it was something I wanted to do, and something that had value.

Maybe someday we'll conjure up some sort of utopian alternate universe in which everyone is handed cash for walking down the street simply because we deserve money for any decision we make. Until then, this is the difficult balancing act of adulthood. Do you want to struggle as an artist, or rake it in as an unfulfilled cubicle slave? Do you embrace the privilege of guiding your child through every moment of his first years of life, or do you go for a paycheck and professional validation? Do you go for a salary—or for benefits?

17

Global Financial Equality for Women Benefits Everyone

Hillary Rodham Clinton

Hillary Rodham Clinton is the United States Secretary of State.

All over the world, women are bursting on the entrepreneurial scene. Investing in their hard work and initiative is good for business and can help women overcome the unfair access to resources they have historically faced. There are many forces working for equality today. International Women's Day in an opportunity to bring more awareness to the issue. An investment in gender equality is not only good for women, but also benefits their families, communities, and the world at large.

One of the biggest growth markets in the world may surprise you. You've heard about the opportunities opening up in countries like China, regions like Asia and industries like green technology. But one major emerging market hasn't received the attention it deserves: women.

Today, there are more than 200 million women entrepreneurs worldwide. Women earn more than $10 trillion every year, which is expected to grow by $5 trillion over the next several years. In many developing countries, women's incomes are growing faster than men's.

Facts such as these should persuade governments and business leaders worldwide to see investing in women as a strategy for job creation and economic growth. Many are doing so. Yet the pool of talented women is underutilized, underpaid and underrepresented in business and society.

Throughout the world, women do two-thirds of the work, yet they earn just one-third of the income and own less than 2 percent of the land. Three billion people don't have access to basic financial services we take for granted, like bank accounts and lines of credit; the majority of them are women.

Certainly we are seeing the impact of excluding women in the Middle East, where the lack of their access to education and business has hampered economic development and helped lead to social unrest.

Throughout the world, women do two-thirds of the work, yet they earn just one-third of the income and own less the 2 percent of the land.

If we invest in women's education and give them the opportunity to access credit or start a small business, we add fuel to a powerful engine for progress for women, their families, their communities and their countries. Women invest up to 90 percent of their incomes on their families and in their communities.

Ripple Effect

When women have equal access to education and health care and the freedom to start businesses, the economic, political and social benefits ripple out far beyond their own home.

At the State Department, we are supporting women worldwide as a critical element of U.S. foreign policy. We are incorporating women's entrepreneurship into our international economic agenda and promoting women's access to markets through the African Growth and Opportunity Act, the Pathways to Prosperity Initiative and women's entrepreneurship conferences.

The U.S. is hosting a special Asia-Pacific Economic Cooperation event on women and the economy to help foster growth and increase opportunities for women throughout the region. We are working with the private sector to provide grants to local non-governmental organizations around the world that are dedicated to women and girls.

Closing the Gap

We are encouraging governments and the private sector to use the tools at their disposal to provide credit, banking and insurance services to more women. Through our mWomen initiative, we will begin to close the gender gap in access to mobile technology, which will improve health care, literacy, education and economic potential.

This is a central focus of my diplomatic outreach. Wherever I go around the world, I meet with governments, international organizations and civic groups to talk about economic policies that will help their countries grow by expanding women's access to jobs and finance.

Many powerful U.S. businesses have embraced this mission as their own. ExxonMobil Corp. is training women entrepreneurs to help them advocate for policies to create more opportunities. Coca-Cola Co. has issued an ambitious challenge in its "5 by 20" program to empower and train 5 million new women entrepreneurs across the globe by 2020.

Improving Access

Goldman Sachs Group Inc. started the "10,000 Women" initiative to open the door for women who would not otherwise have access to a business education. Ernst & Young is tapping into the productive potential of women with its "Winning Women" program to help female entrepreneurs learn growth strategies from some of the most successful leaders in the U.S. Companies all over the world are committed to increasing productivity, driving economic growth and harnessing the power of emerging markets through greater diversity.

As Robert Zoellick, president of the World Bank said, "gender equality is smart economics."

Governments are passing laws that support women's economic empowerment and building awareness of women's rights. Botswana lifted restrictions on the industries in which women can work, for example. Morocco now allows women to start businesses and get jobs without their husbands' approval. Bolivia began a land titling effort to recognize that women and men have equal rights to own property.

This week, we celebrate the 100th anniversary of International Women's Day. It's an occasion for honoring the achievements of women. Without question, the past century has brought astonishing progress, by just about every measure, in women's health, their economic opportunities, their political power and more. Today, women are leaders in every field.

Morocco now allows women to start businesses and get jobs without their husbands' approval.

Acting on Ideas

Never in history have there been so many forces working together for gender equity.

But International Women's Day is also an occasion for recognizing how much more needs to be done to support women and girls worldwide. I encourage everyone reading this to reflect on what you and your friends can do to support women—to put words and ideas into action.

If we decide—as societies, governments and businesses—to invest in women and girls, we will strengthen our efforts to fight poverty, drive development and spread stability. When women thrive, families, communities and countries thrive—and the world becomes more peaceful and prosperous.

Organizations to Contact

The editors have compiled the following list of organizations concerned with the issues debated in this book. The descriptions are derived from materials provided by the organizations. All have publications or information available for interested readers. The list was compiled on the date of publication of the present volume; the information provided here may change. Be aware that many organizations take several weeks or longer to respond to inquiries, so allow as much time as possible.

ACLU: The Women's Rights Project

125 Broad Street 18th Floor, New York, NY   10004-2400
website: www.aclu.org/human-rights/womens-rights

The Women's Rights Project (WRP) was founded in 1972 by Supreme Court Justice Ruth Bader Ginsburg, and it focuses on legal battles to ensure women's rights in education, employment. WRP has been an active participant in nearly all major gender discrimination cases that reached the Supreme Court since its inception; the organization is also committed to advocating for victims of domestic violence, as well as for women and girls in the criminal justice system.

American Association of University Women

1111 Sixteenth St. NW, Washington, DC   20036
(800) 326-2289 • fax: (202) 872-1425
email: helpline@aauw.org
website: http://www.aauw.org/

American Association of University Women (AAUW) aims to advance equity for women and girls through advocacy, education, and research. Since its founding in 1881, members have examined and taken positions on the fundamental issues of the day—educational, social, economic, and political. *Women at Work*, a report by the AAUW Educational Foundation, combines interview and survey data with US census statistics to explore how women are faring in today's work force and what their prospects are for future job success and security.

American Federation of Labor and Congress of Industrial Organizations (AFL-CIO)

815 Sixteenth St. NW, Washington, DC   20006
website: www.aflcio.org

The American Federation of Labor and Congress of Industrial Organizations (AFL-CIO) is a voluntary federation of 55 national and international labor unions. The mission of the AFL-CIO is to improve the lives of working families by bringing economic justice to the workplace and social justice to the nation. America@work, the official publication of the AFL-CIO, is designed to inspire and support front-line union leaders and activists with tips, tools, and news to help build a strong voice for America's working families.

The Feminist Majority Foundation

1600 Wilson Boulevard, Suite 801, Arlington, VA   22209
(703) 522-2214 • fax: (703) 522-2219
website: www.feminist.org

The Feminist Majority Foundation (FMF) strives to develop new strategies and programs to advance women's equality. Along with reproductive rights and access to reproductive technology, the FMF's programs have focused on the empowerment of women in law, business, medicine, academia, sports, and the Internet. The foundation publishes the quarterly *Feminist Majority Report* as well as a newsletter, blogs, fact sheets, books, and videos.

The Independent Women's Forum

Independent Women's Forum, 1875 I Street NW, Suite 500
Washington, DC   20006
(202) 857-5201 • fax: (202) 429-9574
email: info@iwf.org
website: www.iwf.org

The Independent Women's Forum (IWF) aims to expand the conservative coalition, both by increasing the number of women who understand and value the benefits of limited government, personal liberty, and free markets, and by countering those who seek to expand government in the name of protecting women. IWF is a non-partisan, research and educational institution. It produces fact sheets, policy papers and position papers along with a regular blog.

The Leadership Conference on Civil and Human Rights
1629 K St. NW, 10th Floor, Washington, DC   20006
(202) 466-3311
website: www.civilrights.org

The Leadership Conference on Civil and Human Rights is a coalition of more than 200 national organizations, comprised mostly of civil rights and labor advocacy groups. Its website serves as an archive for relevant and up-to-the minute civil rights news and information. Their website, civilrights.org, is committed to educating the public on discrimination in all its forms and features original reports, blogs, newsletter, and an annual publication called *The Civil Right Monitor.*

National Association for Female Executives (NAFE)
2 Park Avenue, New York, NY   10016
email: Roxanne.Natale@NAFE.com
website: www.nafe.com

The National Association for Female Executives (NAFE), founded in 1972, is the largest women's professional association and the largest women business owners' organization in the United States, providing resources and services through education, networking, and public advocacy to empower its members to achieve career success and financial security. The NAFE conference and special events division produces a 100 Best Companies WorkLife Conference, the Best Companies for Women of Color Conference, and the NAFE National Conference. NAFE is owned by Working Mother Media (WMM), which includes *Working Mother* and *NAFE Magazine.*

National Bureau of Economic Research, Inc. (NBER)
1050 Massachusetts Avenue, Cambridge, MA   02138
(617) 868-3900 • fax: (617) 868-2742
website: www.nber.org

Founded in 1920, the National Bureau of Economic Research (NBER) is a private, nonprofit, nonpartisan research organization dedicated to promoting a greater understanding of how the economy works. The NBER is committed to undertaking and disseminating unbiased economic research among public policymakers, business professionals, and the academic community. NBER publications include *Body Composition and Wages, The Evolution of Inequality, Heterogeneity and Uncertainty in Labor Earnings in the U.S. Economy,* and *Long-Run Changes in the U.S. Wage Structure: Narrowing, Widening, Polarizing.*

National Women's Law Center

11 Dupont Circle, NW, #800, Washington, DC   20036
(202) 588-5180
email: info@nwlc.org
website: www.nwlc.org

Since 1972, the National Women's Law Center has aimed to expand possibilities for women and girls in this country. It works to pass and enforce new legislation related to women's issues and its affiliates have litigated cases all the way to the Supreme Court. The Center continues to advance the issues that affect women's lives in education, employment, family and economic security, and health and reproductive rights—with special attention given to the needs of low-income women and their families. The Center's website houses an archive of fact sheets, videos, legal briefs, presentations, and webinars.

National Women's Political Caucus

Suite 425, 1211 Connecticut Ave., NW
Washington, DC   20036
202-785-1100
website: www.nwpc.org

This multipartisan, multicultural organization is dedicated to increasing women's participation in the political field and creating a political power base designed to achieve equality for all women. Through recruiting, training, and financial donations, the NWPC provides support to women candidates running for all levels of office regardless of political affiliation. The organization produces an e-newsletter, which is archived on its website.

Women Employed

65 E. Wacker Place, Suite 1500, Chicago, Illinois 60601
(312) 782-3902 • fax: (312) 782-5249
website: www.womenemployed.org

Women Employed (WE) seeks to make life better for working women. Through advocacy and education, it works toward fair economic opportunities for all women, including better career options and higher pay, more opportunities for training and education, and strict enforcement of fair employment laws. Its monthly e-newsletter, *WE-Zine*, provides timely updates on policy news, WE's programmatic work, and women's employment issues.

Bibliography

Books

European Commission	*The Gender Pay Gap—Origins and Policy Responses: A Comparative Review of 30 European Countries.* Saarbrücken, Germany: Dictus Publishing, 2011.
Warren Farrell	*Why Men Earn More: The Startling Truth Behind the Pay Gap—and What Women Can Do About It.* New York: AMACOM, 2005.
Janet C. Gornick and Marcia K. Meyers	*Gender Equality: Transforming Family Divisions of Labor (The Real Utopias Project, Vol. VI).* London: Verso, 2009.
Nancy Hogshead-Makar and Andrew Zimbalist	*Equal Play: Title IX and Social Change.* Philadelphia, PA: Temple University Press, 2007.
Jane La Tour	*Sisters in the Brotherhoods: Working Women Organizing for Equality in NYC.* New York: Palgrave MacMillan, 2008.
Lilly Ledbetter	*Grace and Grit: My Fight for Equal Pay and Fairness at Goodyear and Beyond.* New York: Crown Publishing, 2012.
Linda C. McClain and Joanna L. Grossman	*Gender Equality: Dimensions of Women's Equal Citizenship.* New York: Cambridge University Press, 2009.

Evelyn Murphy and E.J. Graff	*Getting Even: Why Women Don't Get Paid Like Men.* New York: Touchstone, 2005.
Brigid O'Farrell	*She Was One of Us: Eleanor Roosevelt and the American Worker.* Ithaca, NY: Cornell University Press, 2010.
Thomas Sowell	*Economic Facts and Fallacies,* New York: Basic Books, 2007.
Dorris Weatherford	*American Women and World War II: History of Women in America.* Edison, NJ: Castle Books, 2008.
World Bank	*World Development Report 2012: Gender Equality and Development.* Washington, DC: the International Bank for Reconstruction and Development/The World Bank, 2011.

Periodicals and Internet Sources

BBC	"Female Pay 'Unequal' to Male Colleagues for 57 Years," August 19, 2010.
Stacey Blackman	"Study Examines Male-Female Wage Gap, Post MBA," *US News & World Report,* August 26, 2011.
Mariko Lin Chang	"On Equal Pay Day, Busting 4 Top Myths About the Wage Gap," *Ms. Magazine,* April 12, 2011.
Stephanie Coontz	"It's Not Just a Wage Gap," *New York Times,* April 18, 2012.

Elizabeth Dwoskin	"Why the Argument Against Fair Pay Laws is a Farce," *Bloomberg Businessweek*, June 6, 2012.
The Economist	"Executive Pay for Women," August 31, 2011.
Laura Fitzpatrick	"Why Do Women Still Earn Less than Men?," *Time*, April 20, 2010.
Shaun Gallagher	"Mind the Male-Female Income Gap, but Don't Exaggerate It," *Forbes*, May 21, 2012.
Nancy Gibbs	"What Women Want Now," *Time*, October, 14, 2009.
Huffington Post	"Women Executives Will Destroy the World, Say Male Economists," March 28, 2012.
Anthony Kang	"The Wage Gap Myth," *American Thinker*, September 18 2010.
Glenn Kessler	"Obama's Data on the Gender Wage Gap," *The Washington Post*, June 5, 2012.
Knowledge @Wharton	"The Vicious Cycle of the Gender Pay Gap," June 6, 2012.
Joann S. Lublin	"Coaching Urged for Women," *The Wall Street Journal*, April 4, 2011.
Ashley McDonnell	"Gender Gap in Coaches' Salaries Scrutinized," *The Brown Daily Herald*, November 3, 2011.

June E. O'Neill   "Washington's Equal Pay Obsession," *Wall Street Journal*, November 16, 2010.

Renee Ordway   "Don't Be So Quick to Blame Businesses for Wage Gap Between Men, Women," *Bangor Daily News, June 8, 2012.*

Catherine Rampell   "The Gender Pay Gap by Industry," *The New York Times*, February 17, 2011.

Robert Ross   "Study Alleges Louisiana has Largest Male-Female Wage Gap in US," *The Pelican Post*, December 1, 2011.

Becky Sheetz-Runkle   "Is the Male-Female Wage Gap a Myth? You Decide . . . ," www .womenonbusiness.com, April 20, 2011.

Amy Tennery   "The Real Reason Women Don't Help Other Women at Work," *Time*, May 11, 2012.

Index

G

H

I

J

K